Home is the Prime Meridian

Almanac Essays in Search of Time and Place and Spirit

by

Bill Felker

For Neysa   For Jeni

Bill Felker

Acknowledgements

There would have been no almanacs or almanac essays had Don Wallis not made a place for them in his Yellow Springs News. *"But if you do an almanac," he told me in 1984, "you have to do it every week." With his encouragement, I did and still do.*

In 1995 Al Denman suggested I approach the local NPR station, WYSO, about doing an almanac for radio. He and the station manager helped me get started, and I continue the radio segment I began then, thanks to Neenah Ellis, Peter Hayes and, Juliet Fromholt at WYSO.

I am indebted to the many newspaper and magazine editors who helped me along the way, especially Pat Lanman, Amy Harper, Bob Mihalek,

Diane Chiddister, Jerry Rohrs, Jed Grisez, Trent Gove, Anne-Marie Ida, Cathy O'Kane, Charles Sutton and Nathan Griffith.

And to critic Vick Mickunas, and to friends and family who read through and edited the drafts of my collection, including Jeff Crawford, Judy Davis, Tat Felker, Jill Becker, Anne Shafmaster and Amy Achor.

And to so many others for their suggestions and support, including Ruby Nicholson, Jane Scott, Ray Geers, Matt Minde, Barbara Valdes, Chuck Shows, Kitty Jensen, Robert Johnson, Jane Morgan, Jonatha Wright, Ed Oxley, Maggie Felker, Gordon Chapman, Rick and Mary Donahoe, my parents and my late wife, Jeanie.

TABLE OF CONTENTS

Preface

These essays appeared in an almanac and nature column I have written for the *Yellow Springs News* since 1984 and for my "Poor Will's Almanac" on NPR station WYSO since 2005.

Thinking about events in nature, I have come to see how seasons are not only paths of fantasy and reflection, but also openings to a part of me that I had lost.

I have watched my emotions follow the weather and the foliage and the songs of birds. I have identified with plants, mice, fish, insects and frogs. They have become my teachers.

I have visited Trappist monks, and I have realized through them dimensions of stability and what it means to remain and to grow in one place for a lifetime. I have found that the small town in which I have stayed over half of my life is my own monastic space of meditation and practice.

I continue to find that the more I understand where I am, the more I understand myself. I see how a sense of season and identity necessarily begins with what is closest to me. I find that time and spirit have no scaffolding without home, that home is the Prime Meridian.

Bill Felker

Camel Crickets in the Tub

Camel crickets keep falling into my bathtub-shower in the coldest part of winter. Once there, they hop and hop, but they can't scale the steep, slippery walls that tower above them.

Sometimes these creatures are small. Other times the trapped insects are mature and fat. According to my books, camel crickets can neither hear nor make sounds. They compensate for being both deaf and dumb by having unusually long and sensitive antennae. Young or old, their bodies are fragile, their reflexes sluggish.

But they are obsessed with the smooth, white tub. They creep into the bathroom at night, mount the wooden tub-surround, and slip through the opening between the sliding shower doors. In the morning, I have to scoop them out, take them to the greenhouse, and set them free in the geraniums or begonias. Eventually, they find their way back into the bathroom.

What they are looking for who can tell? For the most part, camel crickets live in basements. They like the damp darkness of caves. The crickets I encounter probably breed in the crawl space under my house and find their way upstairs in the fall and winter seeking warmth.

But that is obviously not everything to know about them. Like the rest of us, they must have secret passions. They have evolved to succeed in a gloomy habitat, but one in which they are safe and nimble. What attracts them to the sleek and fatal receptacle that will not allow their return? Why do they rashly throw their advantage away to explore the treacherous, shining bathtub in which they are helpless?

Are they drawn to the whiteness of the porcelain like moths to the light? Does the bright chasm in the black night promise some forbidden pleasure? Is my tub the great and terrible temptation of camel crickets? Whatever their sin, I feel a certain comradeship with them. They should know better, but they can't help themselves. Their visitations confirm something I know about myself. I share some weakness with them, some deficiency of discretion, and neither they nor I know how to fix the flaw.

Winter Fever

The dark morning sky already prophesies summer: An hour before sunrise, Orion has set. Sirius has moved deep into the west, Cancer and Gemini following it. The Big Dipper is overhead. June's Arcturus is coming in from the east, and August's Vega has risen in the northeast.

This week, the tufted titmice will call. In two weeks, the owls will court, in three weeks the crows will become restless, in four weeks the cardinals will sing, in five weeks the doves will sing, in six weeks the skunk cabbage will open, in seven weeks the sap will run in the maples, in eight weeks snowdrops will bloom, in nine weeks the pussy willows will open, and then the aconites, and then the finches will turn gold. There is hardly time to get ready.

On the other hand, winter fever, like spring fever, short-circuits my concerns. It convinces me to stretch out like my cat in front of the wood stove, to remain unthinking and still, to retreat into the moment, to be here alone and rest and sleep. There is challenge enough to come, the fever tells me: passion, pain, encounter. I should stay here and be safe. Winter is an angel, my body says; hide beneath its wings.

Bill Felker

Looking for Proof

I walk outside to look for proof that spring will really come. October and November leaves have become part of my pathways, worn into the mud. Some moss is growing on rotting logs. Coralberries and black privet berries are still holding. Chickweed and garlic mustard are spreading slowly across the forest floor. The hulls of last June's sweet rockets and August's wild cucumbers are empty, brittle and delicate like shed snakeskin. The Japanese knotweed leaves are hanging like huge russet cocoons. Milkweed pods are stained and empty.

I stand and study the woodpile for a while, trying to estimate how much wood is left. I look in the front garden to see if the snowdrops have come up; usually they have, at least a little, their white tips an easy gauge of earliest spring, even as they push up through the snow.

I look at the honeysuckle bushes, note whether any of their berries are left. I finger the seed heads of the New England asters to see if all the seeds are gone. I kick the fat Osage fruits to understand how they are doing: they are chartreuse green when they tumble down in October and November, turn yellower and yellower through the fall, start to get mushy in the middle of winter, fall apart in spring.

I find the plants that keep their green through the coldest times: the hellebores, the creeping charley, the chickweed and pachysandra, garlic mustard, mullein, sweet rocket, and sweet William, and I am reassured by their deep color and hardiness. I check the buds on trees and shrubs. Hard, scarlet buds on the wild multiflora roses; box elder buds, barely visible, tucked tightly to their green branches; privet buds, minute and black; on the blackberry canes are blood-red buds, their color spreading to the sides of the stalks.

I check the pussy willow catkins; sometimes I count how many are opening. I feel the fleshy, orange buds of the buckeyes; the tight, round, silver buds of the dogwoods, each one marking the tip of its branch; the stiff, woody buds of the crab apples; the pale green buds of the lilac; the sharp and thorn-like buds of the American beech; the deep purple bud clusters of the red maples; the phallic protrusions of the ginkgo.

I measure the gray velvety buds of the white magnolia; the tiny russet linden buds; the yellow-brown, fat sweet gum buds growing beside their dangling fruit; birch buds with their willowy catkins; the buds of the tree-of-heaven, hiding in the hollows of last year's branches; flushed azalea buds protected by their shining leaves: All the proof I will ever need.

Merak and Dubhe

The Big Dipper's Merak and Dubhe, pointers for the North Star, are now positioned east-west after dark marking the midpoint of the calendar year. From that center, I can survey the land and seasons all around my yard in southwestern Ohio. Knowing the average temperatures here, I can gauge the weather anywhere in the eastern half of the country. If I walk east or west from town along the axis of Merak and Dubhe, five hundred miles in each direction, the averages hold to those in my village, dipping slightly in the mountains, rising near the coast. Following Polaris north, the world becomes colder by one degree every twenty-five miles. Going south, guiding on the Dog Star, Sirius, the weather warms by one degree every twenty-five miles all the way to the Gulf of Mexico.

A provincial season, closely observed, is a map to other distant seasons. If I set my watch by the bloodroot in the back woods, that time, with a weather graph or two, will be good enough to make a calendar of bloodroot in a thousand counties. From within the landmarks in this middle kingdom, the outlying areas come into perspective. When I travel through the country in the summer, the canon of my local flora serves me well. I can guide on Queen Anne's lace, milkweed, birdsfoot trefoil and chicory all the way to northern Minnesota, east to

Washington D.C., west past St. Louis, and south into Georgia. The flowers keep me grounded to Yellow Springs as well as mark my way.

And when winter becomes too long, I retreat to my charts. They tell me that between the middle of January through the middle of May, spring moves from New Orleans at a rate of six miles per day or one degree Fahrenheit every four days. The seasons are variable and unpredictable, but those average rates of vernal progress hold. Whatever is lost with one cold wave is gained in a later thaw. When Merak and Dubhe have rotated ninety degrees, pointing north-south instead of east-west, it will be Middle Spring. Hepatica will be old in Tennessee, barely opening in Michigan, full bloom in the middle of Ohio and Indiana.

First Fly

A large black fly has emerged in the greenhouse during these first days of February, and it proceeds to explore the rest of my home, partial to the kitchen and the bathroom.

The family rightly wants the creature dispatched or at least relegated to the out-of-doors. But I am uneasy about killing a harbinger of spring, and the firstborn – under this roof – of the new year.

So far the winter has been gentle; the fly must know what she is doing; she probably forecasts more by her surprise appearance than I could ever calculate with my charts. I am therefore remiss in my duty to get rid of the visitor. Maybe she will just go away, I say.

But as I sit in the greenhouse, typing my newspaper column two hours before sunrise, the fly is not only still here, she has become quite friendly, has taken a liking to me and to my colorful computer screen. She keeps reminding me of my duty to protect her, and of the dire meteorological and personal consequences of any aggression.

She zooms back and forth from my desk to the lamps in two other parts of the room, enjoys the air around the warm wood stove, returns after a few minutes to check up on me. Then she goes off to explore the geraniums, maybe observing the perennial aphids, maybe spying the one or two camelback crickets that have found sanctuary among the flowerpots.

Sometimes she is quiet. Once in a while, she buzzes. At the moment, she doesn't seem interested in contaminating food or spreading germs. She is both coy and obtrusive, elusive and forward. It would be unthinkable that she had nothing to tell me. It is early in the morning, and we are alone. There is no one to see us together. Momentarily free from social expectations and responsibility, I can embrace the first fly of the year without remorse or guilt, smile at her attention, identify with her excitement at being alive in the artificial summer of my tomato and pepper plants, listen for her secret message.

Conversion

In the long cold of the last few weeks, I have withdrawn into a fetal, psychic hibernation, reminiscing about childhood and about other retreats I have made from the weather and the world. This morning, while I was working alone in my attic bindery, listening to the wind and watching the snow, a memory mood from my hermetic high school years at Holy Cross Seminary came back and settled around me.

In my mind, I went back to the seminary crypt under the main chapel, a windowless basement of gray stone, with low ceilings and heavy pillars and pointed arches. It smelled like incense and beeswax. Slab altars lined the walls. The staff of priests, with the students as servers, said daily mass there.

I remembered the sense of complete protection I felt in that place, not only from the northern winter, but from conflicts with peers, hormonal temptations, adolescent ennui. Enveloped in that subterranean chamber and in its ritual, I was the wide-eyed adept. That dim, consecrated cave was the center of my practice, the passageway to the Path. The holy sacrifice which I attended was the ultimate act. The Latin exchange between server and celebrant was the great secret dialogue, the true code, communion with the living and the dead.

Outside the seminary, in the lonely, secular and snow-covered hills above the frozen river, away from sure and scented dogma and hierarchy, there was no salvation. But in the crypt I was safe; I belonged as I have never belonged since. Had I chosen, I could have stayed there forever; I had been born to the elect, and the magical words I witnessed and abetted could change common bread and wine into God.

Then one year, spring came to me while I prayed, and my devotion thawed, and what had once seemed so frightening and alien in winter flowered and sang. My vestments became too tight. Heaven lost its allure. I no longer wanted to be safe or to belong. The hills were green and gold in the sun, and I longed only for the open river and for the magic of earth.

Homely Gnomons

My home in Yellow Springs, Ohio, is a private observatory. Near winter solstice, the sun comes up just on the other side of the Danielsons' house (as far south as it ever rises) and it shines in to the north wall of my home office, reaches high on the west side of the greenhouse wall, lies across the bed in the green bedroom, settles briefly next to the television in the living room.

At spring and autumn equinox, the sun rises directly over Lil's house, shines through my east windows all the way through my office to the west wall of the hall and the living room and the green bedroom, barely strikes the greenhouse at all. And at summer solstice, the sunrise over Jerry and Lee's house (as far north as it ever rises) lights the south wall of my office, and the green bedroom and the living room.

Sometimes I make pencil marks on the walls, with dates of the different intrusions of light. On December 20, I check the line I made years ago that shows how far the noonday sun reaches through my south windows at winter solstice. Sunsets have their own iconography on different walls.

Here the Earth does not circle the Sun. It is the Sun that circles my unmoving space. This house on High Street is the center of the galaxy. It is also a planetary map of my history, with souvenirs following the shadows.

The larger web spreading out from the village is clear enough on the other side of my windows. Through their prism, links of geography and politics, control and purpose fall into place. I filter what I cannot see and understand through my notations on the walls. Grounded in homely lessons, I walk outside if I wish, leaving the prints of gnomons behind, but always remembering where I am.

Counting

Waiting for spring can be like trying to go to sleep when I have insomnia. Sometimes the best thing to do is to count. Counting is a simple measure of time, limits time to individual pieces, takes away its mystery and emptiness. Counting is an act of will, forces focus, works against discouragement, places the counter in opposition to the psychology and physiology of sleeplessness.

Numbers are infinite, and so are the particles of winter. Counting in sequence creates apparent progress and finite limits. Even though awareness of winter's events seems to produce few results and seems to have no sum or substance, observations can be like digits in a sprawling but promising nighttime equation, the fruit of persistence and dogged hope.

Like counting sheep or breaths or numerals, counting dimensions of the interval between autumn and April requires no rules or ethics, is not competitive, does not require special study or skill. Like counting sheep or breaths or numerals, the choice of things to be counted is arbitrary, has no necessary socially redeeming value, does not end poverty or bring peace, has no theology.

This is the anarchy, the freedom that opens the mind's eye to rhythm or accumulation or listing or repetition or the emptiness of objects until something new suddenly occurs without my creating it, and I fall asleep and dream or discover spring.

The Archipelago of Early Spring

In the early spring of the Ohio Valley, islands of new life emerge from the waves of warmth and cold that move across the landscape. Within these islands, often separated from each other by broad expanses of chilling winds, weeks of gray skies, sometimes only narrowly divided by a night of frost, the season reveals its stunning topography.

Early spring is an archipelago of forms rising out of February's great sea, and like ephemeral atolls, the events of this temporal, mottled continent multiply, swell and recede to alter the face of my habitat with an inexorable beauty. The geography of early spring is fixed in shape and order but not in time. The archipelago of winter's end is fluid, what chronologists call a "floating sequence," a sequence the dates of which are relatively well known in relation to one another but not in relation to exactly when they will occur on the brittle Gregorian calendar.

Observation and memory, however, easily decipher the secret code of the floating sequence, uncover the fluid terrain from which fauna and flora materialize and spread a map of promise across the seemingly uncharted expanse of winter. In Yellow Springs, early spring fills the six weeks between the middle of February and the end March. This month and a half links the deep cold with the lushness of April, and it is made up of constellations of color, motion and sound, and musterings of new sprouts and leaves, birds, insects, mammals and fishes. In the South, this season can arrive in the middle of the year's first weeks; along the Canadian border, it comes in May. Wherever the floating sequence begins, it follows something of the order below; no matter where it takes place, the following landmarks are only fragments of a far greater ferment.

Starting with a major thaw well after solstice, the first cluster of spring's appearance takes the form of snowdrops and aconites flowering together in the warmest microclimates beside the prophetic hellebores and Chinese witch hazels of late January. Within a few days, snow crocus and iris reticulata complete this island of time at the chilliest edge of spring.

A parallel cluster rises from the swamps: the skunk cabbage blossoms at Jacoby. In alleyways and lawns, common chickweed, dandelions and henbit complement the cabbage. Above them all, red-winged blackbirds stake out limits. Ducks and geese follow the lead of the blackbirds, marking ownership of the more favorable river sites for nesting. Migrant robins join the sizeable flocks that overwintered in the woods and cities.

Past the seasons of the snowdrops and aconites, midseason crocuses initiate more complex configurations that lead to fat pussy willows, bright blue squills, delicate yellow jonquils, then to the full-size daffodils, then to purple grape hyacinths, to pale wood hyacinths and pushkinias. Towering on the horizon, silver maples and the red maples and box elders prepare to fruit.

To these outcroppings come the pollen seekers: the honeybees and carpenter bees. Other creatures follow. Mosquitoes and newborn wolf spiders look for prey. The mounds of ants rise from winter's prairie. In rivers and ponds, water striders mate. Earthworms come out of hiding, lie together in the mild night rains. It is salamander season in the slime and snake basking season in the sun. Spring peepers peep.

Then the root and insect eaters become active, joining the beavers that have been cutting trees and eating bark since January. Groundhogs dig up the hillsides. Opossums, skunks, raccoons seek their mates and sustenance. Turkey vultures circle the roads looking for road kill. Wild turkeys start to call.

When pussy willows are at their peak, new configurations take shape, adding multiple pathways to all the recent temporal spaces. Into the world of pussy willows come the white magnolias in town, snow trillium along the rivers, spring beauties in the woods. Across the bottomland, soft touch-me-nots sprout, coveted ramps push up their medicinal foliage to pace the stalks of daylilies, rhubarb and precocious bleeding hearts.

When pollen covers the pussy willows, then honeysuckle, mock orange, privet, wild multiflora roses, lilac, black raspberry and coralberry leaves break out from their buds, a signal for *cornus mas* and lungwort to flower and for mourning cloak butterflies and cabbage butterflies to navigate the channels of equinox. A few days later come the question-mark and tortoise-shell butterflies and then the white-spotted skippers.

In the last few days of March when the pussy willow catkins start to fall, the archipelago of early spring becomes a dense maze of islets unimaginable at the end of February. In the trees, the finches turn gold. In ponds, the toads are singing. Calves and lambs appear in the fields. Carp frolic in the rivers. Young opossums come out to play. Wasps crawl from their winter crevices.

In the garden, the early tulips unfold. Star of Holland comes in beneath the bright forsythia. Buckeyes unravel. Plums bloom. And just as skunk cabbage starts to produce its foliage, the first tremendous mass of wildflowers suddenly opens all at once on the farthest and mildest border of the early spring archipelago: inflorescence of periwinkle, hepatica, violet cress, harbinger of spring, bloodroot, Dutchman's britches, bittercress, twinleaf and Virginia bluebell leading now into the endlessly intricate paradise of April.

The Visitor

From time to time, I slide into depressions, sometimes light, sometimes deep. One morning not long ago, I woke up to one of those darker moods in which nothing seemed right or meaningful. Not only was I useless to myself, I thought, but there was nothing positive I could do for anyone else.

Staring out the window and nursing my emotions, I heard the knocking of a yellow-bellied sapsucker on the siding of the house. She had been there before; a yellow-bellied sapsucker had appeared in the middle of spring to tap at my siding nearly every year for more than a decade.

She comes just once a spring on her way to somewhere. If she is not the same bird each year, then maybe a daughter or granddaughter following a family tradition, taught by her parents that for good luck, or maybe for the taste of a certain kind of beetle emerging from the cedar just before equinox, she should stop and check the wood.

And that simple knock, which I would have missed had I been busy at more practical things, brought flooding in the whole optimism of spring. The isolation I'd been feeling dissipated immediately. The bird's presence and her history were all I needed to come back from what seemed to be a hopeless funk.

In my joy, I blew the whole incident out of proportion. I allowed the arbitrary act of a sapsucker to reassure me about the good order of the entire world. Things were not, as my mood had told me, out of sync and empty, but rich and all in place if only I would listen.

Perhaps, I thought, fortune was no more or less than this. Maybe sense and virtue, immediate pleasure and lasting meaning, were as free and as accessible. If the transient yellow-bellied sapsucker could wield the power of happiness, I might have and wield it, too.

Constellations of Middle Spring

In early April mornings, Hercules has moved to near the center of the sky over Ophiuchus, Libra and Scorpio. The Summer Triangle, which includes Cygnus, Lyra and Aquila, is just a little behind him in the east. The Milky Way passes through the Triangle, blending it with autumn's Pegasus rising. The Corona Borealis has shifted into the western heavens, and the pointers of the Big Dipper point almost exactly east-west.

Parallel to these and other celestial forms are constellations of objects close at hand: flowers and birds and amphibians and mammals. Throughout the many brief sub-seasons of the year, such creature reflects the tilt and the spin of Earth.

Earth star clusters of plants and animals, like asterisms made up of distant objects, are fabrications that create seasonal time.

And so after a walk in the woods, one might imagine a Spring Triangle formation made up of red toad trilliums and golden cowslip and bluebells.

Or maybe a Libra-like cluster with four corners: goldfinches in April plumage, bloodroot, morning robinsong and screeching, mating toads.

Or a lopsided, six-pointed, Cepheus-like collection of honking geese and watercress and the first pale spikes of lizard's tail, the flushed, orange bellies of young river chubs, the fattening skunk cabbage leaves and the whistle of red-winged blackbirds.

Or a nine-piece Aquila-like fantasy of daffodils, tulips, serviceberry flowers, pear flowers, wind flowers, buttercups, creeping phlox and new wisteria.

Or a gangly Ophiuchus-like sprawl of morels and cardinals, trout lilies and redbuds, peaches and crab apples, hyacinths, violets and vast patches of dandelions.

In fact, the land of Middle Spring is an immediate firmament, and it is full of bright, soft, fragrant and vociferous constellations. Throughout its cosmic panoply lie signs from which to pluck a treasure of astrological fortune, riches from the neighborhood instead of from galaxies far away.

The Sweetest Way

I have been thinking that if every aspect of the landscape, the immense seasons with their untold stages and creatures, if all those things are shaped by the spin of the Earth and biological clocks, how similar my own changes and progressions must be, all attached to the Sun and the Moon, to heat and cold, prearranged as if there were a cosmic map organic to my brain, as though, like some migrating species, I simply did what I needed to do in order to discover and fulfill my purpose.

Such a scenario seems less a deterministic trap or cage than a self-guiding pathway: perhaps I do not choose this or that action so much as I evolve to see the sweetest way. Like nature, I am looking for the right signs, for the most fruitful encounter. Like a hiker in the woods, I follow the terrain most in tune with my energy, my sense of adventure, my physical capabilities, my constraints of time. Or, like apple blossoms cede to dogwood and azalea blossoms, so I cede to what comes next in this place. My logic belongs to habitat.

Often it even seems that my whole life has been a preparation for one season or another, and that I know exactly and instinctively what I want or need or must have or must possess. And so what might be called freedom or choice is translated into love or into simple awareness of what is most clearly part of who I am.

And so spring in this place (or in my body) could not, barring some catastrophe, be other than an anteroom to early summer. The land and I do what lies within our sequence, not because we are constrained to do it so much as because it is the only sequence that belongs just to us and into which we fit.

In Suspense

The story in fiction promises us a resolution, and we wait in suspense to learn how things will come out.... We are in suspense, not only about what will happen, but even more about what the event will mean. We are in suspense about the story in fiction because we are in suspense about another story far closer and more important to us – the story of our own life as we live it. We do not know how that story of our own life is going to come out. We do not know what it will mean.

Robert Penn Warren, *On Reading Fiction*

April has fallen away so quickly, the trees and the flowers two weeks early, clocking an accelerated movement of the year, measuring in Yellow Springs the power of the great Pacific Ocean currents. The new sweet cicely underneath my bedroom window reminds me that spring never comes fast enough, and when it comes it comes too fast.

The first seasons are a month gone now, bloodroot season, violet cress season, twinleaf season, bluebell season, snowdrop season, snow trillium season, so many more seasons. I have only watched a few of them, and I am thinking about what I have missed. They are fragments of a story, the ending and the meaning of which have always troubled me and set me wondering.

In the way I know there will be a climax to a romantic novel, I know that winter is the inevitable denouement in nature here. I also know rationally that things will turn out for me the way they will turn out for any animal, any flower or tree. Like Robert Penn Warren's fiction reader, I wonder about the seasons and the meaning of the seasons of the landscape because I am wondering about my own seasons and what they mean. I watch them, and I am in suspense because I don't know exactly how they will turn out.

I can see that the life trajectory of plants and toads is just like mine. I can watch and observe as many metaphors on this stage as I can manage, but I do not know if I will ever really come to terms with all the metaphors of brevity, of growth, of passage, of the surge and decline of hormones, and I watch the natural mentors again and come back to them each year to see if they hold something new, and to see something I might not have noticed before.

As an ambivalent Christian, I am drawn to the annual birth of a Savior in the year's shortest days, the winter fasting through Lent and then the defining act of Easter, but firm faith and understanding elude me. Each year, I see the story enacted. I know Christ will be born only to be crucified, only to rise again triumphant, and I never know quite what that means, and so I follow the cycle one more time.

Each year, spring overpowers winter, finds fulfillment in the summer, teaches all the lessons of the beauty and the power of procreation and decay, is sealed in the tomb of December only to rise again triumphant. I watch the story every time as if it might be my own story, but I am never quite sure that it is, or do not know why it is or how, and then when the plot unfolds all the way, that is never quite enough, and so I start over. I read the book again. What will it say this time?

Bill Felker

Notes on the Northern Spring Field Cricket

At the beginning of early summer, the Northern Spring Field Cricket begins to sing in Ohio Valley pastures. This cricket is the easiest of all the crickets to identify because it is the first and only species to appear at the end of spring. Overwintering as a nymph, it comes out as the canopy closes, when rhododendrons, peonies and mock orange bloom, and the first strawberries ripen.

By the middle of July, when the other crickets are just starting their seasons, the Northern Spring Field Cricket has completed its cycle. By then, writes Vincent Dethier in his book, *Crickets and Katydids*, "the crickets of early summer, have sung their lays, courted, consummated their love, and died. Their consorts have laid eggs in the soft soil and died in turn."

As autumn approaches, the number of cricket species multiplies, and the task of identification becomes more challenging. Entomologists like Dethier have found that the shape of a cricket is less helpful in naming its species than the insect's call. "Appearances," he writes, "are neither distinctive nor meaningful, but an acoustical signal to which the female can orient and home is essential. And the song must be correct in order to lead the female to the genetically compatible mate, otherwise consummation, even if completed, is fruitless."

Like Dethier, I find little use for outward appearances as I reflect on the subtle differences in the species of men and women. There is, I think, something radical and violent that separates us, either some vastly complex design, or else a primordial mix-up that once set our evolution out of kilter, a cosmic banishment that scrambled our voices and scattered us like children of Babel, and in order to find our partners and friends, to break the isolation and loneliness, to be fruitful, we have to sort through a planet of neighborhoods and habitats. We have to study where we might belong if we are really ever to find home, and then we have to listen and listen and listen until we hear the one song meant only for us.

Strawberry Summer

A wave for the sea,
Flower for fruit and fruit for tree,
A part for the whole,
A kiss for the soul,
Ambrosial lips: you for me:
Strawberry synecdoche.

bf

Those interested in classical letters might be familiar with the figure of speech called synecdoche (pronounced sin - EK - deh - key) in which a part of something is used to refer to the entire object – or vice versa. In natural history, this verbal device is even more useful than in literature, an isolated flower or scent or taste easily able to conjure whole seasons, call up memories that cross lifetimes.

In early June, strawberries are a single tip of summer. But with synecdochic power, their odor and flavor expand time and space, envelop a totality of events in their maturity. With strawberries come the longest days of the year and the completion of the forest canopy. The planting stars, Arcturus and the Corona Borealis, are overhead at night, Hercules not far behind them to the east, followed by the Milky Way, middle summer's Vega and the Northern Cross. Scorpius follows Libra across the southern sky.

One ripe strawberry implies all of the flowers of early summer: chamomile, clustered snake root, white clover, red clover, yellow sweet clover, yarrow, blue-eyed grass, angelica, prairie false indigo, hemlock, blackberry blossoms, wild roses, swamp iris, meadow goat's beard, feverfew, blueweed, black medic, daisies, wild mallow, fire pink, water willow, motherwort, white campion, parsnips, honewort, moth mullein, heliopsis, quickweed, lychnis, astilbe, swamp valerian, moneywort, scarlet pimpernel, catalpas, meadow rue, dogbane, sundrops, privet, spirea, poison ivy, tea roses, Miami mist, spiderwort, snow-on-the-mountain, day lilies, bindweeds, thistles, sweet Williams and crown vetch.

Strawberries are a sign that mulberries and pie cherries are getting ripe, black raspberries not too far behind them, a sign that quail are whistling for their mates, that box turtles are laying their eggs, that spiders are weaving their webs across forest paths, that the spring field crickets are mating, that fireflies are glowing, that silver-spotted skipper butterflies visit the garden, that maple seeds fall, that May apples are an inch across, that cattails and yucca stalks are as tall as my chin, that timothy is ripe for chewing.

The catalogue of objects and events could go on and on. And not only is each term in the list convertible from part to whole, from microcosm to macrocosm, the psychic possibilities for reminiscence and fantasy contained in each evocative fragment outstrip any kind of organization or reason. Overcome with the chaotic convergence of synecdochically-charged spirit and matter, I reel under strawberry summer, feel lost, elated, nostalgic, confused, sad, excited, lonely, in love, full of regret and optimism.

Bill Felker

Journal on Crows and Thomas Merton and Butterflies

The other night, the wind blew hard across the village. I lay awake for a while and worried about the aging Osage orange falling into the shed or crushing Jeanie's favorite redbud tree, maybe reaching the new porch and taking out the past summer's work.

This morning before sunrise I am sitting on that porch; we all survived the storm unscathed. The sky is clear deep blue. The robins have been singing for more than an hour; cardinals and doves just joined in a few minutes ago. Now the shining grackles come through the high trees, gliding from their secret nests; cackling and clucking, they move down among the black branches.

When I first came outside, I looked for light frost on the grass, but the lawn was wet and dark. Now it reflects the glow in the east behind me. The air is humid and still. Crows call to the west, and I hear the crows I hunted as a child in Wisconsin. They were wily, untouchable crows, and they watched me from high cottonwoods until I stepped within maybe a city block of them, and then up they went screaming.

I open the journal of the monk and author Thomas Merton that I have been reading this past week, captured by his journey toward death. It is still too dark to make out the words.

I think about one of the things Peter Matthiessen learned from the *Tibetan Book of the Dead*, that "a man's last thoughts will determine the quality of his reincarnation." I am coming to the last year of Merton's life. I want to see what he was like in those last days. I want to read his last thoughts. Of course, my own last days and thoughts are what really concern me.

But when it is finally light enough to read, I am taken in a different direction. I am pulled by the sunlight spreading down the locust trees that line the far edge of my property. I close the journal, and I watch and wait for cabbage butterflies and the first bees.

The Pond

Several years ago, my wife and I dug a small pond in the back yard. With fish and plants, it has been a successful and rewarding habitat. What surprised me about it this summer was that, with its maybe seventy-five square feet of surface, the pond satisfied all my youthful passion for much larger bodies of water.

When we made a short trip along the Southern coast early this June, we walked a little on the beaches. As I looked out over the curved blue horizon, I felt none of the great longing I used to feel when I visited the shoreline. Now I realized how impossible that vague dream of the water had become, how inaccessible the adventures, the infinite variety of creatures. I was disappointed that the thrill of the sea had disappeared before I had taken enough time to embrace it.

Then a few weeks ago, I sat by the pond, surrounded by the flower garden of lilies and zinnias and spiderwort and heliopsis. I fed the four tame koi, enjoyed the light breeze and watched an orbweaver spider spinning its web above the lily pads.

I knew that I now preferred this small pool to any ocean. Here was a place within my power. Here was wildlife enough for me to watch. Here the fish ate from my hand. Here were just a few water plants blooming on their own schedules, plenty to keep track of, plenty for measuring time.

The horizon was not the globe's ever receding promise. This world was flat. This distant shore was accessible, and I could actually touch it. My reach for once did not exceed its grasp. I gave in to this attainable sea, its borders as fixed and finite as my own.

Stilling the Kinematoscope

Keeping notes about events in nature over a number of years has shown me what I already knew: if something happens once, it will usually happen again.

When I see a particular insect or flower for the first time in the year, I check my daybook to find when I saw it in other years. Sometimes things are early, sometimes late, but they are almost always in the right sequence, the variations dependent on the quality of the season.

Often, however, I assume too much and go too far. When I see the same things happening every May, I develop expectations, and when those expectations are fulfilled, I take the expectations a little further, and then a little further still. I pretend to find rules and systems.

Finally, I start imagining that not only is each day's journal a record of its own events, but a history of what has always occurred and what will occur again and again. I no longer wait for repetition in order to formulate patterns or predictions. One day's narrative becomes enough to defuse the need for replication.

Instead of the effect sought so diligently in the 19th century by the creator of the kinematoscope, in which still pictures were rotated or manipulated to create the illusion of motion, I find a reverse effect in multiple images and in repetition, an inverse kinematoscope that stills the disruption of passage.

Once I reach that point, everything makes sense. I settle in to the solid landscape of here and now. One event reaches back and forth through multiple seasons, is knit tightly with parallel events that are separated only by time, time that, in spite of appearance, and no matter how fast it seems to fly, makes the present only more fixed and indelible. Nothing is separate. One event is all there is.

Free Lepidoptery

Today, I am watching butterflies without an ulterior motive. I am done with trying to identify and count them, have given in to my confusion about their names and markings and their meanings.

Rum and cola in my hand, I have put aside my lepidoptery, or, closer to the truth, I have chosen to purify it of its purpose. The butterflies, after all, seem to come from nowhere, appear and disappear like fantasies or daydreams. I know too little about them to be scientific or to draw objective conclusions about their habits. Their temporal and spatial borders are uncharted for me, and it is an easy step from curiosity to procrastination, from studying to distraction and sloth.

The afternoon is full of sun, and the breeze is cool. The chasm between observation and wasting time, which seemed so wide just a little while ago, has collapsed around me, and my sense of application and utility, of duty and obligation and responsibility, has been unplugged. The butterflies' passionate, fluttering search for sweetness and brightness is teaching me to draw no conclusions, to avoid the issues at hand, to forget the inevitable, to embrace excuses, to postpone commitment, to put off until tomorrow, to pretend, even to avoid indifference or nonattachment or anything wise or virtuous or transcendent that might lead to enlightenment or wisdom or knowledge.

Freed by my ignorance and lassitude, I have nothing to gain from the butterflies. I can do nothing with their bodies. I cannot capture their souls. These particular butterflies do not balance the planet, nor can I see the hurricane their wings may now be stirring in the Caribbean. I cannot connect their dots. I cannot feed the hungry with them, clothe the naked with them, cannot visit the sick with them or bury the dead with them. They dance in front of me without Jesus or the Buddha, without salvation, without heaven or hell, without sin or virtue, without selfishness or magnanimity, without humility or kindness or goodness or evil, without history or the future. Floating among these disconnections, I delight in liberty, am pure and clean and loopy, untied and clueless.

Angels in the Woods

Unlike simple geographical locations, which exist objectively, places do not exist until they are verbalized, first in thought and memory and then through the spoken or written word.

Kent Ryden, *Mapping the Invisible Landscape*

Today is so hot here at the monastery, the humidity so high. But I go for a walk before the sun gets higher and I get too tired.

A reading from Genesis at the service this morning: Abraham's wife, Sarah, had mocked the angels (disguised as travelers) who had promised her she would bear a son in her old age. Of course, against the odds, the child appeared.

I wander out into rolling hills, past new hay rolled into great round bales, into patches of tall violet monarda and knapweed full of honeybees, bright orange butterfly bushes full of butterflies, white Queen Anne's lace and yarrow, long drifts of daisy fleabane, the pathway lined with sky-blue chicory and vervain.

I ruminate about Kent Ryden's assertion that place or landscape exists only as a projection of the mind, that the land is not only dependent on our perception but takes its nature from what we formulate its shapes to be. Place is structure that seems so separate and distant but is actually inside us, constructed by us, an outcropping of our vision.

After an hour in the sun, I retreat into the dark and the shade of the forest. I accept the cool and the mosquitoes. The middle summer woods provide only fragments of color: a few avens, a lost fleabane, one pale wild petunia, some small yellow sorrel, but sassafras, pawpaw, locust, walnut, yellow poplar, creeper and sycamore offer me their protection.

I walk past the religious sculptures placed along the walkway every few hundred yards: a Virgin Mary, a St. Francis and other storied figures. I ponder the written requests that visitors to the monastery have placed at their feet. I consider prayers and miracles. Then at the end, I come across three angels disguised as statues. Landscape as the figment of my mind: what will those three promise me?

Ladybugs at the Beach

Jeanie and I were sitting at the beach at Saugatuck along Lake Michigan, three hundred miles northwest of Yellow Springs. The wind was cool and the sun was hot, and we dozed and read and dozed and stared out at the clear blue, blue sky and water. In the distance, sailboats moved across the horizon, and seagulls bobbed in the waves.

Things were all in order. Lovers walked hand in hand along the shore in front of us. Children built sand castles. Fathers raced with their sons, and mothers huddled and chatted with their daughters.

Once in a while, a horsefly landed on one of us but then flew off without biting. Sometimes when a cloud covered the sun and the wind grew colder, three or four common black flies would take refuge on my jeans. In the course of the afternoon, butterflies came by, swallowtails and viceroys, their explorations light-hearted and playful.

In the middle of the afternoon, a ladybug landed on the novel I was reading. Not wanting to accidentally crush the insect, I gently pushed it off. Ten minutes later, it – or one like it – was back on the pages of my book as though trying to tell me something. I brushed it off again, but it returned again a little later, apparently in trouble, the fine beach sand sticking to its fragile wings. I got up and took it to the dune behind me and set it on a blade of grass. It fell upside down to the ground beneath, and then I noticed that there were ladybugs everywhere.

Some of them were regular lady beetles with two or nine spots; others had no spots at all. But most were the pale brown Asian variety, the kind that appears throughout Yellow Springs in late summer and early fall.

Unlike all the other creatures at the beach, all of the lady beetles were clearly having problems. They were the most numerous creatures along the waterfront, but they were the least prepared to deal with that environment. And it also seemed they had no purpose for being there.

Landing or falling on the wet sand, they hobbled awkwardly toward the lake. When small, gentle waves spun them around and set them up higher on the beach, sometimes the ladybugs would turn around and head right back to the water. Sometimes, they tried to escape toward land, racing in the direction of a low mound only to be swept up and turned upside down by the pursuing tide. They seemed stupid and brave, helpless and blind, determined and dogged, unready, clueless.

Were they really playing like the butterflies and the children? Were they migrating? Had they crossed vast Lake Michigan on some high wind only to be dropped here on the sticky sand? What did the great architect of the universe have in mind for them here and now?

The activities of the gulls and the horseflies I could explain and anthropomorphize in order to pretend to recognize their function. I could see their activity on the beach as purposeful and focused. I could see the play and courtship and relaxation as making sense.

But then the absurd fate of the ladybeetles, the futility of their struggles, and my lack of understanding began to color the way I saw the rest of us at the beach. Instead of the false sense of comprehension, the hollow peace of finding each thing in its correct place joined by proximity on the great canvas of the lake and sky, I began to see our overwhelming lack of connection. Horseflies and children and lovers and I were all arbitrary and random objects, brought here together by motives so deeply distinct: the heart of the sailor out a mile from shore so distant from my own heart, the boats and the beetles all solitary and separate.

As the sun cooled and the wind grew stronger, I moved from the morning's sense to the afternoon's nonsense, taking things at face value, resigning myself to their chaotic influence, which was, after all, the very purpose of a day at the beach: pattern, design, control, explanation, context all unraveling as I let go of my spiritual reins.

The ladybugs' predicament unlaced my remaining ties to logic and causation and reasonable cosmology, laying bare my actual disconnection and my empty proximity to boats and families and butterflies. At home when I am busy making sense, putting things in order, finding purpose and meaning, lining up my notes, I lose all sight of truth.

The End of Robinsong

I am up before five in the morning., sitting on the back porch, waiting. The waning night is cool, and I have my jacket hood up like a monk before Vigils.

From the middle of March through the day before yesterday, robins chanted at this time, a persistent, singsong chirping. This morning, like yesterday morning, everything is quiet.

The gibbous Moon lies overhead, weaving pathways through the lattice of the porch, leavening the sky for sunrise.

I have been so accustomed to the robins' presence, to their routine and to their purpose. I strain to hear their song, but it is not there. Each year their silence is timed so precisely, almost to the hour, their reading of the sky so exact. Even though I know better, I feel empty, as though none of this will ever come again, as though in this sudden turn of July something irreparable has occurred.

Compensating, I sort through other impressions. From the half darkness, shapes slowly appear in the garden, the wheelbarrow full of cut grass, the three bird feeders, the birdbath. I can finally see the words on the page of my notebook. I feel my ears getting cold.

The Moon shadows fade, and the first cardinal sings at 5:40, the first dove at 5:45. Then cars join in along Dayton Street. The eastern sky grows brighter, and everything seems to be the way it should be. A neighbor's cat with white feet and chest moves across the yard as though I did not exist. The impatiens in the window box take on their purples and reds by 6:00. In the garden, individual flowers appear from the darkness, orange and violet day lilies, the first red dahlia of the summer.

The cardinals grow louder. Mosquitoes start to whine around my face and hands. I gather up the new voices and colors and put them in the space of robinsong, filling in the absence until finally I regain my balance. Then more quiet as the sun strikes the back trees, and the cardinals and doves fall silent, predicting the end of their nesting and mating in August. Crows at 6:37 as though nothing were out of place. A blue jay at 7:17.

Watching Romuald

"Sit in your cell as in paradise," stated the 11th century monk St. Romuald. "Put the whole world behind you and forget it. Watch your thoughts like a good fisherman watching for fish. Empty yourself completely and sit waiting, content with the grace of God, like the chick who tastes nothing and eats nothing but what his mother brings him."

A green frog named Romuald lives in the pond near my house, and he doesn't seem to mind that I watch him. When I am sitting on the bench close to the pond, he will jump right up on the stones I have placed around the water's edge, and there he will remain motionless and without affect, betraying no emotion as long as I care to stay. Although I sometimes hear him croak in the night, he is always quiet when I am watching.

For a while, I waited to see if my frog would actually do something. Maybe he would catch a fly, I thought, or dive in after a piece of fish food that was floating by. But the frog soon taught me that there was nothing to do.

If I were a naturalist, I would stay by the water as long as it took to know exactly what this frog ate and where he slept, and really how long he could stay out of water and how far he could jump. If I were a scientist, then I would learn all of those things and more and then draw conclusions and give a paper.

But Romuald is teaching me to leave the world of reason and specifics behind, and so I am free to contemplate the frog in itself. I can rest lightly in his impassivity. He is, after all, in his cell. He appears to be empty, content, waiting for the grace of paradise.

Talking the Walk

It seems to me now that the spin of the world is speeding up, that time is moving more quickly than it did just a month ago. It seems that the entire year is collapsing around me, and that there is still too much left to feel and do.

I struggle to find footholds with which to keep my balance in time. I want to understand everything that is happening to nature and to me, but I get distracted by thinking and trying to know, and then I lose my place and fall away from the path.

Of course, there is nothing except the summer itself if I simply talk the walk. Only words make the world. Nothing exists outside the reach of a voice. I look at the ground and turn it into truth: two ants, a clump of grass, a dandelion gone to seed, a housefly, a mosquito near my foot, a broken twig.

If I pause or stop or wonder or wish or want, the real summer becomes longings and nostalgias and regrets.

So I pull myself back and talk the walk again: the black walnut fallen to the street, the fat Osage fruit thumping to the back garden. I exercise the discipline of litany in listing events, trusting that events in words accumulate, that more and more and more will be enough.

This is wishful thinking, I am well aware. It

is nervous chatter that distracts me from what might really lie behind the shortening of the days. Memory and hope are the vultures of the word and the present. They rip and tear the flesh of my litany, my summer chant. But if I can just walk here without stopping, without looking back or ahead, I will keep my balance. I will talk and talk the walk.

Kiser's Journal

The other day, a friend of mine handed me an old school notebook, seven inches by eight, paper cover torn and pages yellowed.

"You write almanacs," she said. "You might be interested in this."

It was a journal by the late A. Z. Kiser from Springfield, Ohio. His record contained notations in pencil for every day between September 1950 and December 1952, and it included temperatures, barometric highs and lows, and a general description of each day as "fine," "cold and wet," "hottest yet," and so forth.

When conditions were a little unusual, Kiser added a few words to his observations. The 19th of November in 1950 had the "first snow to cover the ground." Six days later: "a blizzard – 24 inches of snow – stopped the busses. No cars moving, city emergency declared, no one allowed up town."

Kiser kept his fishing diary in the journal, too: September 6, 1950: "no keepers." September 9, 1950: "two keepers."

He also mentioned baseball and football scores, like on October 3, 1950: "New York 1, Philadelphia 0." On January 1, 1952, he "saw picture on TV of Rose Bowl game for the fist time. Michigan 40, Stanford 7."

Kiser wrote down other incidents without placing any particular emphasis on one kind of event or the other. For example, on February 22nd, 1951, he "planted a pot of glads in the cellar." The next day: "Frank died." Four days later: "Seen first two robins in the yard this year." May 3, 1951: "Best mushroom year I ever heard of." Late that summer, on August 1: "Great grandson was born today." The next entry: September 4: "First paw-paw of season."

In November of 1951, these three entries: November 8: "Eleanor went to work, fainted and died before she reached the hospital." November 12: "Eleanor's funeral today at 10:30 a.m." November 15: "I got one rabbit. H. (Kiser's friend) got two pheasant, one rabbit."

Kiser collected "almost three quarts of night crawlers" on March 29, 1952. On April 16, he "had first rhubarb and got 81 mushrooms." On the 20th of that month, he "got run out of woods." (I assume he was trespassing in search of mushrooms.) On April 21: "Caught the largest rainbow trout I ever seen, 2 lbs 10 ounces." On the April 27: "Over 100 people here for 50th wedding anniversary."

The election of 1952 went like this: July 11: "Ike was nominated on first ballot, and Nixon was nominated by acclamation for vice president." July 28th: "Went with Bill to hunt groundhogs. Saw 3, got none." August 15th: "Got about 60 night crawlers." September 2: "Mary made five quarts grape juice and five glasses of jelly." October 9th:

"Put up the stove today." October 17: "Dug glads today." November 11: "Ike just cleared the way to White House at 12 midnight."

Now maybe A. Z. was a man of few words, and maybe he really knew which things mattered and which things didn't. Or maybe the notes were arbitrary and had nothing to do with his values. Or maybe his daybook told it all and put things into lineal perspective.

I ask myself: Was Ike's election as meaningful to Kiser as the gathering of worms? Were the funerals of Eleanor and Frank more important to him than hunting groundhogs? Was the 50th wedding anniversary more significant than putting up the stove?

The journal doesn't say. Kiser was evenhanded. He left no clues. All his entries seem to be made with equal pressure on the pencil, and their style is as lean as their content.

I am also a keeper of notes, and I think about my own selectivity in what I record. From my daybook, one might assume that all the sightings of birds and insects, all the counting of blossoms and the dating of wildflower bloom are more important to me than my family or any other aspect of my life. I wonder, sometimes if they are, and if that is true, I wonder how such a thing could be.

Kiser teaches me to see. Hierarchies of events can skew the story, can twist the memory of what really happens. To be even-handed: that is the Path.

Talking Mosquito

…how you stalk and prowl the air
In circles and evasions, enveloping me…

D. H. Lawrence, "The Mosquito"

Sometimes in the mornings before sunrise, I am a shadow boxer. I evoke my studies from years ago, passing studies in the martial arts, and I play with the forms I once knew, imagining an enemy attacking from the shadows. Up until the other day, no one had ever tested my solitary skills.

As a child, I was a Boy Scout, and I spent many summers at camp, progressing through the various degrees of proficiency offered by that organization. At one point, I was inducted into the Order of the Arrow, a national Scouting honor society, and at the end of an initiation period, each of the chosen was given a special name.

At that ceremony, the older boys received their insignia and honorary names first. I remember a tall and muscular eighth grader being christened Running Buck. Another strapping young man was called Brave Bear. Someone else, a wiry, athletic kid, was given the title of Fierce Eagle.

The elders approached me, shook my hand. Henceforth, I would be known as… Talking Mosquito.

Talking Mosquito!

My heart sank. I fought back tears. What kind of fearless warrior had a name like Talking Mosquito!

Then the other morning, some fifty years or so after that summer, I was shadow boxing in the yard. The sun was still three-quarters of an hour below the horizon, and the east was clear, the crescent Moon rising, red Mars setting behind me.

I was swaying slowly, almost ceremoniously in the twilight, following the scripts of my martial forms, when out of the dark trees came my opponent, obviously intent on drawing blood.

I could see her outlined against the pale golden sky, and I heard her singing as she came – talking, actually, because she was clearly a talking mosquito, and she was keeping back no secrets, calling me by name, apparently aware I had lived in ignorance and disappointment for so long.

I moved quickly to engage her, but that was madness, for the nimble attacker simply rose into the air and stung me lightly on the back of my hand. I brushed her away, and this time she taught me to keep my interval and to watch my breathing. She trained me not to strike too quickly or she would disappear, not too slowly or she would take me.

Back and forth we went, her slender body here then there, always telling, always teaching. Gently but relentlessly, the mosquito guided me through my basics: centering, blending, leading, timing, yielding, following, sticking, coiling, always sensing the other, never too hard, never too soft.

Until the sun rose bright over the tree line, and I walked out from the shadows and entered the real world of normal intercourse with conventional opponents and partners.

Which lessons did the teacher come to show me, lessons of childhood or of aging? Something of both, of course. Most of all, she reminded me of my name and of who I was and still might be.

Bill Felker

Self-Deception

It is often late September when I make my trip into Kentucky to meditate for a few days at Gethsemani monastery.

I rarely see the monastery at any other time of year, and my trip takes me out of the linear context of the world of Yellow Springs in which I normally live. When I arrive for my retreat, the same flowers are always in bloom, the same trees are turning, the same birds singing. Nothing has changed since the last time I came. Time has been held still by place.

At home, I find no such stability. Every day, the markers of the year change just a little. The anchor is pulled up with each sunrise. Nothing stays the same. But at Gethsemani, like a childhood memory of home or a distant summer of love, like an old photograph revisited, or a repeating dream, the season remains frozen to its context.

Before dawn, the sky spreads so deep above me, Orion always at the same stage of his ascent in the east, the Pleiades always overhead. Away from city lights, the sky is so dark and clear that I can always see the legs of Taurus, not just his red eye like here at home, and the Milky Way is almost as bright as a Moon.

Inside the chapel, the sun falls through the tall stained glass windows at the same angle at Vespers as it did last year and the year before and the year before. The solar clock has stopped here, has not passed through winter or spring or summer.

I too am the same year after year, always looking for the same answers, never coming full circle, always staying suspended in autumn, never finished. Maybe that is well and good. I will die, after all, in the world of circles, within the whole turn of some near or distant year. But in the few hours of retreat, I step outside the loop, hide from the inevitable, stand still in self-deception.

Inventory in Early Autumn

A cardinal sang a little after seven o'clock this morning, sang off and on for about an hour. Crows came and went. Sparrows were chattering outside in the honeysuckles about eight o'clock, hummingbirds at work at the feeder.

When I walked the alley after breakfast, I heard starlings whistling and chattering toward downtown. Sitting in the greenhouse, working in the middle of the morning, I listened to the tapping of a yellow-bellied sapsucker on the siding of the house, an old friend returning from spring on the way back to Tennessee. As I left for the woods, a long, long flock of grackles flew southeast, leading the way.

The sky was so clear, the wind soft. I went out beside the water, taking inventory to keep the day: great fields of goldenrod at the height of bloom; the first white small-flowered asters; new chickweed sprouts with two to four leaves spreading across the ground; bare buckeye trees with new buds showing; aging smartweed and snakeroot; blanched wood nettle; seeded wingstem, leaves mottled with powdery mildew.

I saw summer-green ginger leaves; gray brome; dry leaf cup; agrimony seeds crumbling; wood mint dry, still fragrant; field thistles puffed; burdock brittle; the last tall coneflowers and the last lobelias and last woodland sunflowers and last orange jewelweed; new beggarticks; fresh burr marigolds bright as April cowslip; the low, low river; a downy woodpecker "chirr" and blue jay bell call and kingfisher rattle and nasal "peent" of a nuthatch and a robin peeping its migration song.

Crows followed me home. There, the climbing virgin's bower still held its blossoms on the redbud tree. The white boneset and the zinnias and New England asters filled the north garden, and cabbage whites and monarchs and painted ladies, buckeyes and red admirals, fritillaries and checkerspots and skippers and swallowtails, honey bees and bumble bees still swarmed around them. Jumpseeds along the front sidewalk still jumped when my fingers stroked them. Craneflies were spinning in the sun. Dragonflies still hunted in the backyard pond. The koi still fed with gusto, their water almost as warm as it had been in July.

The Monks of Ellis Pond

One autumn Sunday morning, I took part in a walking meditation at a local park, Glen Helen. After instructions about how to do this practice, the participants set out in a line to follow the leader. We walked very slowly and silently.

Hikers and lovers and families with children moved by us quickly. I had joked before the walk how we all should wear long robes so that people might know that we were meditating, but, in fact, I didn't need a robe to feel separated from the non-meditators. I cocooned inside the file of walkers.

Two days later, I took my ancient border collie, Bella, for a short outing to Ellis Pond, a small lake a mile from my house. The wind was quiet and the water smooth at the approach of the remnant of Hurricane Patricia. The ash trees and sugar maples were bare, the sycamores three-fourths empty. On the far shore, the cypress foliage was rusting.

When I was about to leave, I looked over toward the arboretum's grove of oaks to see if they were shedding. That was when I saw the geese. Out of a cornfield they emerged, two or three abreast, solemnly waddling at about the speed of walking meditators, their plumage like monkish habits, gray and white (except for the one white goose that always stayed with that flock), forming a long, formal anserine procession.

The file passed by the brush and shallows at

the northwest end of the pond and plodded toward me where the bank was not so high. When the leader reached the edge, it remained there for a moment as though taking stock of the slope of the land. The others stopped behind it, not breaking ranks. When their guru slid gracefully into the water, each meditator in turn pondered, decided, followed, at least five dozen of them I counted, and they swam out single file in silence.

These were, I assumed, the same seemingly secular geese that fed and mated and raised their young in the field across from the park, the one white tagalong goose pretty much clinching my guess.

And I knew that these birds flew back and forth sometimes, and gathered in the nearby fields sometimes and had loud conversations and quarrels. And I knew that geese liked order and formations. But I didn't know their cenobitic fellowship was also marginally monkish and that their occasional practices included moving contemplation, their liturgy as disciplined as that of dharmic seekers in the Glen.

Promises

If you are afflicted with melancholy at this season, go to the swamp and see the brave spears of skunk cabbage buds already advanced toward a new year…. See those green cabbage buds lifting the dry leaves in that watery and muddy place…. They see over the brown of winter's hill. They see another summer ahead.

Henry David Thoreau, *Journal,* October 31, 1857

In spite of the calls of geese that urge me to abandon the cold, I am spending winter in the North again. I have done my raking for the year. The strawberries are covered with straw. The pumpkins are aging, and the apple cider is made. The garden is filled with manure. Sweet Williams, spinach and onions are planted and covered for April.

With summer scattered and withered, I count each of my allies, from my wife and daughters to the birds at the sunflowers. The tropical plants I have inside the greenhouse are budding, needing care and reminding me of choices I have made. It is too late to run, to merge into the flyway corridor away from January. I am committed to equinox.

After the nostalgia that accompanies the departure of robins and the sadness of leaf fall, my brain receives new signals, defiance and a call to survive. I am already counting days, attempting to demystify the time ahead. Thirty-five days to solstice, 65 to the center of winter, 100 to the first hours of early spring. A finite, divided winter is already mastered. Soon it will seem too short, I tell myself, the hibernation not long enough.

The foliage of May's sweet rockets is already waiting all across the woodland floor. The worst freeze will not kill it. There is a faith in its roots, a knowledge I can use against my suspicion that the end of the year mirrors too closely the end of human existence. Far wiser things than I have absolute faith. They give promises the sun has and will come back again.

Storms and the snows arrive to test the woodpile and my fantasy of self-sufficiency. The corner is turned. The grieving for summer and fall is quickly over. In a few weeks, it is no surprise to see bare branches. I look for what is there instead of what is gone.

Christmas cacti blossom. Aloe spikes rise to flower in the late November greenhouse. Paperwhites send up foliage. My violet hibiscus blossoms, remembering some tropical dictate, finding just the right amount of light to make its seeds. In the sun, the starlings, staying here within reach of my safe feeder, swing in the back trees. Window parsley is growing new leaves.

I go out collecting second-spring foliage from sweet Cicely, chickweed, sweet rockets, waterleaf, cinquefoil, violet cress, hemlock, parsnip, avens and next September's zigzag goldenrod. There are days when it could be March, hazy skies, cardinals singing, temperatures in the warm fifties.

I walk the swamp and find Thoreau's "brave spears of the skunk cabbage, buds already advanced toward a new year."

"They see over the brown of winter's hill," Henry David promises me. "They see another summer ahead."

Bill Felker

The Jug of October

A fixed duration of time is a bounded region on a path along which an observer moves. In short, a duration of time is, in this metaphor, conceptualized as a container.

George Lakoff & Mark Johnson,
Philosophy in the Flesh

The canopy of leaves appeared solid throughout the hot summer, its entire nature dense and uniform, its shade thick and deep. Within a few days, that canopy will shatter. If I accept the philosophers' time as a container, autumn is a jug into which and during which all the leaves come down and all the last flowers fall. In such a scenario, October is not so much a part of an astronomical sequence as it is a bounded region in which I live.

Everything from the whole year past goes into the jug of October. Events and objects get mixed up in the tumble. The smooth wall of June is torn apart. The best sense of what I am in this place dissolves. All of the long, green horizon crumbles.

Any meaning that an observer might have associated with the middle of the year is recast. The change of appearance is the change of essence. The undoing of the trees and flowers tips the full glass of summer to empty, pours out old and familiar landmarks and gauges and pointers all at once.

Untied from the tight landscape of warmth and color, the contents of October's jug have no geography recognizable from August. Nothing looks the way it used to look. The inner space contains pathways but no direction or destination. Nothing linear matters because there is no place to go until the container is filled to the brim, then overflows and tumbles, empties and is free for spring.

Autumn Samadhi
Counting absences
Days without red-winged blackbirds:
Autumn Samadhi

bf

The inventory of middle autumn is rich in foliage and color, but the approach of late autumn draws down the density and texture of the canopy and strips away almost all the floral barriers to winter.

In the same way that spring overcomes February and March with an accumulation of new growth, fall spreads across the summer with an accumulation of loss. I count what no longer holds, make an inventory of emptiness, cued only by memory and the more durable, woody scaffolding that binds the seasons:

Leaves are down from apple trees and crab apple trees, ginkgoes, sugar maples, trees of heaven, redbuds, black walnuts, catalpas, box elders, locusts, elms, birches, poplars, cottonwoods, peach trees, cherry trees, Osage, red oaks, white oaks, chinquapin oaks, sycamores, red mulberry and white mulberry trees, sweet gums, silver maples, Japanese maples, beeches, magnolias, mock orange, silver olive shrubs, honeysuckles, hydrangeas, Korean lilacs, quinces, privets, viburnums, burning bush, dogwoods, spireas.

Silent mornings: no more robins chattering, no cardinal song, no dove song, no red-winged blackbird song, no grackle song, no cicada song, no katydid song, no cricket song.

Hollow milkweed pods, bare raspberry canes, bare blackberry canes, the leaves of hostas and stonecrop melted, innumerable flowers absent and harvest complete: no wheat, soybeans, corn, tomatoes, peas, beans, cucumbers, zucchini, lettuce.

From a litany of creatures and events no longer present, I unthink the world, take it down and let it rest. Emptiness is to space what silence is to sound. In the monastic embrace of the quiet, autumnal cell, I watch and listen, counting absences, replacing nothing.

Winter Tomatoes

At the end of July, I planted winter tomatoes for the greenhouse. I put in a package of the imported Shirleys (thirteen seeds – fifty cents a seed), a dozen Big Boys, and a half a dozen Gardener's Delights, a small early variety.

My greenhouse lies behind a south wall, twelve feet of glass tall, twenty-eight feet wide. When clouds permit, the sun shines on most of the plants from the middle of the morning until three or so in the afternoon, even on the shortest days of the year.

Tomatoes are tolerant of winter light. Given a good start outside in the summer, they begin to climb by the beginning of October. They are over my head by the middle of November, reaching up to the top of the first tier of windows, shutting out the bare branches of the hedge outside and the neighbor's house. I let their suckers go where they choose.

By December, the plants have risen to ten feet, and when I sit in the wicker chair beneath them, they shade me from the sun, and they dapple the moonlight on the brick wall behind me.

At twelve feet, their peak in January, they are peerless allies, angels whose soft wings protect me from the winter. Grown flat up against the glass, they are a living barrier, an insulation of spirit as well as a gauge of a certain balance I keep with the world. Neither I nor the tomatoes were meant to last beyond a predetermined threshold. Our alliance is a fantasy that will blacken and wilt if something goes awry..

Now late at night, in the center of a storm, I sit in the thrill of that dark and peril, and I listen to the wind, and I wonder at the strength and fragility of the tomatoes. As the snow builds up on the windows, I wonder at our ingenuity, our ephemeral beauty, and our reckless defiance.

Retreat at Solstice

This they tell and whether it happened so or not I do not know; but if you think about it, you can see that it is true.

Black Elk

Always in search of seasons and seeking a retreat at solstice, I spent the Christmastide at a monastery, where all the seasons are taken very seriously.

Now that I am back, people ask me what it was like to leave family and festivities for silence and solitude. I tell them that the isolation seemed to speed up psychological time and allowed me to process so many thoughts and feelings. And the more I took part in the monastic rhythm, the more I realized that I was becoming part of an elaborate and deeply layered mystery play about higher time, part of a celebration of God on Earth.

So, imagine a majestic theater in a castle, surrounded by many thousand acres of hills and lakes and woods. And imagine that a company of men – think of them as actors or monks or whatever you want to call them – puts on daily performances from 3:15 a.m. until 8:00 p.m., a total of eight each day, year around.

These performances are like acts of an immense theatrical production. The acts have names: Vigils, Lauds, Mass, Terce, Sext, None,

Vigils and Compline. They are highly complex compositions that follow the seasons of the year and change with them. They are choreographed to perfection, always start and end as scheduled, include readings, songs and psalms, and the actors chant their most important messages like some kind of Greek chorus.

Now imagine all of this, and make one adjustment to the theater analogy. These actors believe that their play is reality, and that the story they tell is true, not only historically but also existentially – so that they spend all of their lives together in community, celibate, in costume and dedicated to that repeating seasonal drama, putting it on over and over again decade after decade, trying to perfect it and trying to live their most authentic selves within it.

Imagine a little more: The theater is almost always full. An audience comes from all over the country and even from overseas to watch as well as to become participants in some of these performances for a day or longer. Each person attends and observes and takes part in a different way, trying to understand what is happening, trying to follow the plot, taking advantage of the intermissions, which sometimes last three or four hours, to walk in the woods, to reflect and read and meditate on the story and their lives.

People wonder where I stand on all of this.

Am I a partisan of this troupe's message? Do I believe their tale? I have to admit that for me the line between a suspension of disbelief and belief itself is a very porous line, and that my identification with or love of certain characters in a book or play often crosses over into my life.

Great stories are almost always true, whether they "happened so or not." Grace is subtle. Narratives cut many ways. By the time I returned home to Yellow Springs, my questions about reality and the semblance of reality were no longer meaningful. As a spectator, I had unwittingly joined the drama, and now I practice my part.

The Green Ladder

A screech owl was calling this morning when I opened the back door at 6:35. Walking the dog a few hours later, I was surrounded by the songs of robins, starlings, sparrows, cardinals, doves and titmice. I stopped to talk with Peggy, who said she'd never seen so many robins in winter. I felt the same way: I've seen overwintering flocks in Yellow Springs for years, but the number of robins seems different this year.

Thanks to a mild December, snowdrops and a few daffodils are up at least two inches in the yard. Small new hollyhock leaves have opened in the garden. Purple deadnettle has expanded into mounds under the grape arbor. Along the sidewalk, about a dozen pussy willows have cracked just a little. By the trellis, honeysuckle berries, which sometimes measure the advance of spring as they disappear, are completely gone.

At the Covered Bridge, I found foot-long growth of feathery hemlock leaves. Some rose hips were soft and squashy; some were brown, brittle, hollow. Osage fruits, some reddish, some still yellow, had been shredded by squirrels or raccoons, lay all about the forest floor.

The deeper I went into the woods, the more I noticed the moss around me, and I realized that almost all the stones were green, that the fallen logs were green, that the rotting stumps were green, that the oldest trees overhanging the river were covered with the thickest, most luxurious green moss, fat and bushy, an inch thick in places. Dry streambeds were filled with green rocks and branches.

Everywhere I looked, islands of summer shone through the dead leaves, and it drew my vision through vertical pillars of green up into the blue sky.

This Advent, I have been reading essays by theologians Thomas Merton and St. Bernard. Both of them obsessively extracted novel and often useful meanings from the events of the Christian liturgical year. St. Bernard was especially gifted at enumerating things such as the three aspects of Advent or the twelve rungs on the ladder of humility. In his lists, he explored so many unlikely dimensions of a topic, often reaching well beyond the expected to achieve his desired number of insights.

As I walked, I wondered what Bernard would do with all these verdant Scriptures. He was a man who made tiers of everything, filled in the empty spaces of events, created sequences out of concepts, found allegory wherever he looked. I imagined him without his Jesus and without his Church, helping me to see what really lay before me. I imagined him building the green ladder of this day, finding four transcendent stages in deep winter, six hidden levels in the thickness of mosses, nine miraculous shades of January jade, twelve secret dimensions of the living stones nestled among decaying leaves, fifteen lessons in the enigmatic deer paths that cut carpets of bright chickweed into geometric icons, twenty symbols of inner life growing from the ancient tree stumps, thirty signs of resurrection in the crossed branches of the hoary sycamores, all the meanings I ever needed flowering from Gaia's Word.

Bill Felker

Feeding Birds

Sometimes the day is quiet, and not a single bird visits the yard. Sometimes the sparrows invade and feed all day. Other days they follow a fractal sort of pattern, eating in fits and starts, the lawn and bushes full of sparrows then empty, then full of sparrows again then empty. When the sparrows move elsewhere for a while, cardinals, titmice, chickadees, wrens, blue jays and nuthatches take their turns. Recently starlings and doves have joined them.

Sometimes I make notes about which birds I hear singing and which birds come when and how they act: the sparrows, like starlings, staying tight to the motions of the flock; the acrobatic chickadees swooping in and out, remaining only seconds to grasp their sunflower seed and fly off; the wary, fluttering titmice; the blue jays, harsh and bullying; the hopping, syncopated nuthatches exploring upside down; the heavy, pushy, long-billed starlings; the slow and awkward doves; the cautious cardinals feeding in the twilight; the crows that never land here but are present with their calls before dawn.

I do not follow a birder's schedule. I have lost my life list. I know only with glimpses, know with parts instead of wholes. But watching birds, I watch my feelings. I can see that there is an emptiness inside me without the birds, a completeness and odd security in the presence of the birds. When I forget to feed them, they withhold their consolation. Bribed with seed and suet for their company, they offer comfort and reassurance.

Notes on a Community of Koi in Winter

When I was younger, I enjoyed fishing and the excitement of discovery that accompanied it. I sometimes killed the fish I caught, and my mother would fry them for me. As an adult, when I caught, prepared and ate fish, I felt self-sufficient.

Now that I am old, I have a pond and four large koi. The fish have names: Buh buh (orange and white) and Bud (black and white), Princess (silver and black) and Golden Shark (gold and black). Last summer, they produced almost two-dozen fingerlings, kaleidoscopic in color.

Over the years, I have fallen in love with the ways of my koi: their caution and their eagerness, their loose hierarchies and their mutual support, their gentleness and their occasional spurts of excitement.

When the water warms above sixty degrees, they are active and swim freely. They come toward the edge of the pond when I approach with their food. The larger fish seem only mildly competitive, allowing the young to eat first if they choose.

In the winter, the cold seems to slow them all into contemplation. They move close to one another below the remnants of the lily pads. When I approach, they remain quiet, usually side-by-side, sometimes tucked together as though they were keeping each other warm. The fingerlings have a separate spot beside the lily roots, clustered like the adults in cenobitic security.

In this artificial sea, aerated by a pump and waterfall, climate controlled by a pond heater, the inhabitants lie out of danger, waiting for spring. Caring for them, I turn away from the violence of my own youth and of my species. I pretend that all is well. I make believe that the peaceful community of winter fishes is the real world and that some benevolent caretaker watches over us all.

The Whole Nature of the Wynde

....thereby I might se very wel, the whole nature of the wynde as it blewe that daye. And I had a great delyte and pleasure to mark it, which maketh me now far better to remember it.

Roger Ascham

I am up at six sitting in the greenhouse. The sky is half dawn, light and dark equal through the fast gray nimbostratus clouds and the storm. The wind is hard from the southeast. The pattern of the gusts and rain creates a shape of its own, harsh like pebbles or hail, then soft, sweeping and blending, retreating.

After a few minutes, quiet. Then more squalls come pelting the house, surging at me passionately, pushing towards my chair, the sound measuring the speed, the size and quantity of the force. The most savage attacks shatter the raindrops against the window. My excitement increases with the intensity of the pounding that almost becomes too fervent, and I am growing restless kept at this high climactic plateau.

Then the pressure suddenly eases, the cloudburst ends. I can see the tall cottonwoods swaying a block away, and instead of the wind given voice and revealed by the rain, instead of its insistent drumming and clattering, I hear it rushing in the bare branches and singing in the crevices and corners of the buildings and the fences around me. A few feet from where I sit, chickadees dive and hang at the feeders, glide with the rhythm of the air, at ease in the swells of the wind.

A small leak in the roof lets an intermittent drip of water fall on the indoor plants. The intrusion keeps a different time than that of the wind and rain outside, measuring how warm and dry and still I am here, surrounded by yellow pine and old brick, with a fire in the wood stove, and red and lavender geraniums and impatiens, all the silent warmth of summer collected and safe.

The Magic of Christmas

I am a child of Earth and Starry Heaven,
But my race is of Heaven alone.

Orphic Verse from the Petelia Tablets

Christmas approaches, and I get ready to go through the traditional practices of selecting and wrapping gifts, setting up the tree, helping to decorate the house. The first candle of the Advent wreath is burning as I write. Like many Christians, I wait for the rebirth of God and the land.

The natural year has put a clear end to the last leaves, garden greens and flowers. The nights are the longest of the year, and the days are gray. The sun lies at its cold solstice declination.

Evenings by the fire, I have been reading about the ancient Orphics, pre-Socratic Greeks whose ceremonies contained secret rituals that guaranteed safe passage to everlasting life. I have been reading about Dionysus, who died and rose again, and about Diana of the Ephesians, virgin earth goddess, distant antecedent of the Virgin Mary.

Many Sunday mornings, I attend mass. One of my favorite verses urges the congregation to come and take the body and blood of the Lord, the food and drink of immortality. I eat and drink, and I give in to all the rites of the season.

Still, I am always uneasy at this time of

year, especially vulnerable to phobias and doubts. Who can tell if the sun will really move higher in the sky after solstice? Who can know for certain that Earth will really tilt back toward spring? Who really knows if I am immortal?

Like the Orphics, I am afraid. I need a secret formula. Bypassing the cerebral cortex, my heart and limbic sense tell me I had better place my bets on liturgy and mystery.

In winter, the outside world is so indifferent. I build up the fire in my wood stove. Would-be child of Earth and Starry Heaven, I indulge in reckless magic and faith in Heaven alone.

Mice in the Mug

Wee, sleeket, cowran, tim'rous beastie,
O, what panic's in thy breastie!
Thou need na start awa sae hasty,
Wi' bickering brattle!
I wad be laith to rin an' chase thee,
Wi' murd'ring pattle!

Robert Burns

I keep my birdseed in a plastic container inside a small shed behind the house, and the other morning I forgot to put the cover back on the container.

When I went out to feed the birds the following day, I discovered at the bottom of the near-empty container, a mouse peering out from the coffee mug I used to scoop the seed. Its nose was quivering like a dog's, and its eyes were huge and black. It had fallen into the container, hulled numerous sunflower seeds, but then had been unable to climb out.

So I took the container outside to dump the cup and mouse and feed the birds. But when I looked down once more, a second mouse appeared from out of the cup and then a third: three fat, frightened mice packed into a coffee mug, coming out to look at me and then retreating back into the highly inadequate shelter, stuffing themselves so tightly that only their tails stuck out.

I stood in the snow, imagining their panic and their dread. Certainly, they might have known I was their adversary. I had killed so many of their kind in traps winter after winter when they had invaded my porous house to find warmth and crumbs. They had little reason to hope for clemency.

But the more I thought about what they might be feeling, the more I became entangled with myself. Shamelessly I anthropomorphized those mice, projecting my own fears and regrets upon them. Suddenly their predicament stood for all the foolish, reckless, thoughtless, ill-advised things I had ever done in my life, things so stupid that I try to forget them all the time but never quite succeed.

I made a general confession of my failures to the mice, telling them things I had hidden for so long, admitting to them things I could not have told a human soul. And it felt so good, talking to these compatriots in crime, that, for just a moment, it seemed a fearsome burden had been lifted from me and that my transgressions had been absolved.

Slowly I reached down and lifted the cup, spilled its contents close to a space under the shed where the mice could escape. They stood for an instant in the sun and the snow, their pelts shining, priestly dark, their fat, black eyes searching mine, then scurried for safety.

"Go and sin no more," I told them (and

myself), placing a little extra seed around the hole into which they disappeared.

For a few days, they were on their best behavior. I decided that they must have understood all I told them, that they had learned from their mistakes and mine, and that they had realized, as Robert Burns wrote, how "the best laid schemes o' Mice an' Men,/Gang aft agley,/An' lea'e us nought but grief an'pain,/ For promis'd joy!"

Then yesterday, I found a small hole gnawed into the side of the seed container near the tightly fastened lid. This time, there were four mice in the mug.

Bill Felker

Inventory at New Year's Eve

The year seems to pause as the sun lies within a few minutes of solstice, but the landscape continues to be the sum of my observations. Like every other season, winter in this place accumulates, is only what I see it to be, is all that I see it to be.

So once more I take inventory in the alley and the yard: grasses pale and bent; hulls peeling and unraveling on the black walnuts; some Osage fruits nibbled by squirrels or raccoons; hoary goldenrod and great ragweed broken; blackened euonymus drooping; chicory twisted; burdock leaves collapsed and brown; pokeweed hollow and empty; garlic mustard, sweet rocket, tall ragwort, celandine, poppies and thistles still green but limp from the cold; empty small white and New England asters; *stella d'oro* foliage splayed; brittle lily stems; chives flat and pale; only a few parsley stalks still standing. And I have not begun to see.

Bill Felker

Home is the Prime Meridian

When I am restless, the landscape around me doesn't seem enough, these few acres of woods and houses just a taste, only a promise of the great world.

But when I go too far out, I need to gather my landmarks of home around me. Distant locations only make sense against my local gauge.

Time benefits from a master point like Greenwich; from that arbitrary marker, one can know the sun throughout the world, make maps, even plot the instant and the physical place where the past and future blend to a single day and balance in a temporal vacuum.

Even if I do not live in Greenwich, I know that its longitudes follow the sun through the entire globe. In a similar way, place has no scaffolding without home. Home is the Prime Meridian. So if I know who and where and when I am in my neighborhood, I also know my time and location and identity everywhere.

The winds across my land are not only parochial. The hills above the paths are not barriers. The river, disappearing around the last bend, goes out to the end of the world, proceeding from and returning here.

Bill Felker

Bill Felker has been writing *Poor Will's Almanac* for papers and magazines since 1984, and he has published annual almanacs since 2003. His radio version of *Poor Will* is broadcast weekly on NPR station WYSO and is available on podcast at **www.wyso.org**.

For more information, visit Bill Felker's phenology website at **www.poorwillsalmanack.com.**

Bill Felker

Bill Felker

70749124R00073

Made in the USA
San Bernardino, CA
06 March 2018